We
Speeches
and Jokes

Other titles in this series:

Wedding Speeches and Jokes

Barry Wogan

foulsham

LONDON • NEW YORK • TORONTO • SYDNEY

foulsham

Yeovil Road, Slough, Berkshire SL1 4JH

ISBN 0–572–01591–7

Copyright © 1990 W. Foulsham and Co. Ltd

Printed in Great Britain by Page Bros (Norwich) Ltd

Contents

Foreword

You have to make a speech at a wedding and you are nervous. Unless you are a practised public speaker it can be worrying to stand up and address a company that probably includes many strangers.

Take heart. It is not difficult to make a wedding speech. Your audience is already warmed up by the happiness of the occasion. They do not want a long speech, they do not expect an important speech, and high oratory would be out of place.

What you should give them is a few sincere and perhaps amusing words. This little book shows you how.

Presenting Your Speech

All the speeches at wedding receptions are really toasts, and replies to toasts.

The first, to the health of the bride and bridegroom, is made by the bride's father, or an old friend of the family where the bride's mother is a widow. The bridegroom responds for himself and his new wife, and then proposes the second toast, to the bridesmaids.

Oddly enough the reply to this toast is made not by one of the bridesmaids, but by the best man on their behalf.

At formal weddings no other speeches are made, but at more informal receptions the bride herself is often asked to say a few words, and a sort of second proposal of the health of the newlyweds is sometimes made by a practised and witty speaker.

The main thing to remember about any speech at a wedding breakfast is that it must be brief, certainly not more than four or five minutes at the very outside.

And the best speeches are often shorter still.

Do I read it or learn it?

There are various ways of presenting your speech. You can write it all down and simply read it out. You can memorise it completely and then recite it like an actor. You can memorise the main points, perhaps with the aid of some brief 'headline' notes, and then speak off the cuff.

The first method is disastrous; your speech will sound like an announcement about the next train over the station loudspeaker.

The second is better, but inflexible. It will not

allow you to comment on some little incident of the day—the black cat that crossed the bride's path this morning perhaps.

The third way is best of all. Your speech will have a shape that has been carefully worked out, and yet you can fill in that shape as the occasion demands, or as inspiration suggests, when you come to deliver it. It is these last minute additions which can really bring your speech to life.

Don't worry if you have not spoken in public before. A couple of practice runs in front of a mirror, and perhaps a close but critical friend, will give you confidence. Remember too, that your audience will not be too demanding. A wedding is a happy occasion, and no-one either wants or expects serious oratory.

How should I speak?

The way in which you speak is very important. You must never sound pompous or patronising and, believe me, it is only too easy to seem both when you are speaking on your feet.

On the other hand, don't be too informal. A wedding, even a highly informal one, is an important occasion, and your manner should show that you recognise this fact.

You must judge for yourself just what your manner should be. Your audience will almost certainly be made up of some people you know very well indeed, and some people you hardly know at all. Remember the ones you hardly know at all. To them you are a stranger, or a comparative stranger, and they will not expect you to address them with too much familiarity. They may come from a background in which a greater degree of formality than that to which you are accustomed is the norm. If this makes your audience seem a rather daunting group, always remember that they are at the wedding to enjoy themselves and will be tolerant of inexperienced speakers— but not rude or over familiar ones.

Generally speaking you should avoid formal words and phrases, which will sound either boring or pompous, or both.

However, you should also avoid slang. This is partly because it detracts from that 'sense of occasion' I talked about, partly because some of your listeners will not know what you are talking about.

Nothing dates as rapidly as slang, and since your audience will be of a wide variety of age groups, a good slice of them will be either too young or too old for your particular slangy useage.

Never swear—not even damn or blast—and never be blasphemous. This is not because most people will be offended; they won't. But because just one might be, and you have no right to spoil a happy day for that one person.

When it comes to pronunciation, always use your natural accent. Never try to talk with a refined, posh accent if this does not come naturally to you. Just talk to the wedding guests in the same way that you would talk to a family friend who had dropped in to visit you.

But this does not mean that you can be sloppy about your pronunciation. Make an effort to sound your d's and t's and h's clearly, though without overemphasising them. Consonants at the ends of words can get lost, especially when the next word starts with another consonant. For example, if you want to say 'that time' or 'and did' properly, there must be a tiny pause between the words. The best way to avoid this particular pitfall, which is good advice to many inexperienced speakers, is to speak just a little more slowly than you do in normal conversation.

Everyone knows the old advice to speakers: stand up, speak up and shut up. Well, the most important of these is speak up, without a doubt.

You simply must be heard, or there is no point in making a speech at all. Nervousness often makes a speaker inaudible. So does an unaccustomedly large room. Nor should you assume that the presence of a microphone will make matters any better! If you have never used one before, do try to get some practice, and if this is absolutely impossible, ask advice from someone with experience—there are tricks to it. Also, make sure that there is somebody on hand who will know what to do if the system begins to whistle, squeak or otherwise misbehave. Prompt action can avoid a most embarrassing pause in the proceedings.

The simplest thing, however, is often the one that drowns the beginner: he simply forgets to breathe. He forgets that in normal conversation he hardly needs any extra breathing effort to make himself heard. Besides, conversation is normally a dialogue. You get a rest in between sentences while the other speaker has their say.

When you are making a speech, there are no little pauses like this—unless you make them yourself. So, you must make them. Don't try to hurry. Say what you have to say at a leisurely pace, and don't hesitate to pause quite heavily between sentences, or even between phrases if you want to.

Another important thing to remember is never to try to compete with extraneous noises. When you first stand up there will still be a small babble of conversation, perhaps the clinking of glasses being put down, or the noise of chairs being pulled round to face you. You must wait until these small noises have died down and you have your listeners' full attention before you start.

When you have it, jump straight in. If you can start with a joke or a witty remark, so much the better. That will get your audience laughing and on your side, and eager for more.

How should I stand?

If you are not already an accomplished speaker, don't make gestures as you speak unless they come quite naturally to you. There is nothing worse than watching a speaker flinging his arms around like an opera singer. It detracts from the speech, for who can concentrate on the words when the speaker appears to be trying to swat a mosquito?

Where do you look when you are making your wedding speech?

Well, not at the floor, and not at the ceiling. And not constantly at your notes if you have any.

If you are proposing a toast, you should look in the general direction of the subject of your toast. But don't stare fixedly at them, or you will look like a dummy in a dress shop window, and embarrass them into the bargain.

Let your gaze move around a bit. And when you mention someone who is present, turn to look at them—with a smile.

What do you do with your hands? Some speakers like to grip their coat lapels, but this tends to give them the appearance of a course bookmaker shouting the odds. Others lay their hands flat down on the table, and rest their weight on them, but I cannot recommend this either. The pose this time is of a shopkeeper waiting for a customer.

Do whatever comes naturally. Notes can come in useful here, because even if you don't ever refer to them, they give you something to hold.

The best speaker I ever heard put his hands in his pockets. From the point of view of good manners it was no doubt unforgivable; but he felt happy talking in that way, and because he felt happy he spoke well.

There are certain things which nervous first time speakers all too often do, and which should be avoided at all costs. Do not clink loose change or keys in your pocket—it is distracting and irritating. Do not loosen your tie—remember that this is a formal occasion, not the third form straggling out of school. Do not mop your face with your handkerchief—it is simply not nice!

Remember that your audience will probably be seated while you are standing, so direct your head down a little towards them. Don't droop like a wilting daisy, just incline your head a little down. Try not to shuffle from one foot to the other, or to rock backwards and forwards. If you put your feet slightly apart and stand upright but relaxed, you will feel more comfortable, and you will look confident.

Should I tell a joke?

The art of wit cannot be acquired in a few weeks, however hard you practice. Nor will you succeed in sounding witty by either learning or reading someone else's script written specially for the occasion. A natural or professional comedian's success lies in the ability to act, in facial expression and in the confidence that comes with assured popularity. Few ordinary people possess this talent. If you are one of the lucky ones who do, you will be well aware of your ability and will need little help. If you are not, do not even attempt to make a wholly witty speech. The result will be both painful and boring!

However, there is no reason why you should not tell one, suitable, joke. Indeed this will help to relax both you and your audience. Twenty years ago a wedding reception was considered no place for comic stories. But times change, and even at the grandest weddings these days the funny story or amusing quotation is quite acceptable.

What is important is that you must not tell a vulgar joke, not even a vaguely risqué one. Think what a nervous strain the day has been for the bride and groom, and reflect how an unsavoury story could embarrass them on this very public and important occasion.

In the same way you must never embarrass the newly-weds with references to their honeymoon, to any previous marriages or liaisons, to the family they may or may not have in the future, or to sex in any form. However funny your anecdote or joke may be, this is most definitely neither the time nor the place to tell it.

What you can do to raise a laugh is to make fun of yourself, of your shyness, of your inadequacy as a public speaker, of the fact that at least twenty other people could do the job better than you. But you must not make fun of the bride or groom, or any other guest except the best man, who is fair game for a little gentle raillery so long as there is obviously nothing viscious behind your words.

What should I say?

Like every properly constructed speech, a wedding speech must have a beginning, a middle and an end.

You can start by saying that you never made a speech before—though you should avoid that terrible cliché, 'unaccustomed as I am to public speaking'. This will get the audience on your side. But of course you must not say this if they know perfectly well that you have been orating all over the place for the last twenty years!

Another good way to start your speech is with your carefully chosen joke or amusing story. This will immediately set a pleasantly relaxed tone and ensure that your audience is really sitting up and listening.

When it comes to the serious content of your speech, it is most important to remember that you are proposing or responding to a toast, or both. I have heard speakers so carried away by their flights of oratory that they have sat down without performing this basic duty—to say the only thing you really have to say.

It is quite simple. If you are proposing the toast you simply say at the end of your speech: 'I ask you to rise and drink the health of. . . . .' or some such words.

If you are responding the words need not be quite so formal, but you must make it perfectly clear in your opening sentences that you are thanking the company for drinking your health.

A simple 'thank you very much' is often surprisingly effective. Other formulae you might use are 'I (or we) thank you most sincerely for your kind wishes . . .' 'It was most kind of you to drink my (our) health . . .' and so on.

When it comes to rounding off your speech of response, it is quite acceptable to repeat your thanks for the toast that has been drunk, thus avoiding any need to think up a clever ending.

To sum up then: your wedding speech must be brief, it must be audible, and it must do its job of proposing or responding to a toast.

Checklist

☐ Plan and rehearse your speech

☐ Write 'headline' notes on a card

☐ Check microphone beforehand if at all possible

☐ Do not drink too much before your speech

☐ Make sure you have a glass of water to hand

☐ Stand relaxed but upright

☐ Remember to breathe

☐ Do not talk too fast

☐ Stick to what you have to say

☐ Relax and enjoy yourself

Notes

Specimen Speeches

Toast to the bride and groom

This is normally proposed by the bride's father. If the bride's mother is a widow, the toast should be made by a relative of mature years (an uncle for example) or an old family friend.

The toast should be brief. About three minutes is adequate, five is plenty, more than five too long.

The exact content of the speech will depend on the relationship of the speaker to the bride. However, it will normally include four important elements.

Firstly the speech will indicate the happiness that the speaker has had in seeing the bride grow up from delightful child to beautiful and talented young woman. A brief anecdote from the bride's childhood may be included, provided that it is in no way embarrassing.

Secondly the speaker will want to say how happy he (and his wife) has been in getting to know the bridegroom and his family.

This leads naturally to the third point—the confidence felt in the couple's future together. Here it is acceptable to add some short and amusing piece of advice from an 'old hand'.

Finally, and most important of all, comes the toast itself. It may be a good idea to decide on the actual wording of your toast, even though the rest of your speech has been extempore, since this is not the moment to suddenly find yourself lost for words.

*　　*　　*

Specimen 1

'Ladies and Gentlemen—I see a lot of happy, smiling faces around me today, but no-one looks quite as happy as the two young people on my right. Just look at their faces! They say marriages are made in Heaven, and while this may be true of most marriages, it certainly is not true of this one. This marriage was made in my drawing-room, eighteen months ago when I introduced Robert to Jean. I remember when I was helping my wife to do the washing up afterwards—that's a pleasure you have to look forward to, Robert—she said, "I think Jean's taken a fancy to that young man." I paid no attention, of course, but when, six months later, Robert asked my advice about engagement rings, I had to admit she was right. When your daughter gets married and leaves home they say, to cheer you up, "You're not losing a daughter, you're gaining a son." In my case I'm also gaining a telephone, I think, but if I may be serious for a moment, I could hardly wish for a better son-in-law than this young man. He's a handsome chap, you'll agree, and I know he will make Jean the perfect husband. No, not too perfect, I hope. That would be a little dull, and married life ought to be exciting, a sort of adventure. I know mine has been. As for Jean, well, she's a bit of a bargain if I may say so, though I won't say she's entirely without faults. (I'll have a word about those in private, Robert, if you like, a little later). I know, and you know that these young people are going to be blissfully happy. Let us stand then, and raise our glasses to them, and make them this wish in the words of the fairy tale: May you live happily ever after.'

Specimen 2

'Ladies and Gentlemen—I read in a newspaper the other day that marriage was going out of fashion. Of course you can't believe all you read in the newspapers, but if they were right—well did you ever see two young people so delighted to be out of fashion? Brides are supposed to look radiant, and bridegrooms are supposed to look clean. Well, Jean is certainly the most shining bride I've ever seen; you almost have to shield your eyes to look at her. And Robert *does* look clean. He looks as if he's been scrubbed behind the ears with a hard brush. Perhaps he has—I know they had some pretty useful gifts from you!

'Anyway, they both look marvellously happy. Your wedding day is supposed to be a bit of a nervous strain, but I've seen no sign of it from these two. In fact just a moment ago Robert leaned across to me and said: "Do you think it would be all right if I slipped a slice of that cake in my pocket?" I had to remind myself then that he is of age to get married. It seems only a few months ago that he was coming home from school with frogs in his pocket! I must say he's found himself a fine girl in Jean even if she is my own daughter. My wife agrees with me. Indeed as we came out of the church she turned to me and said, "She'll make something of him." There you are Robert, you are warned. You are going to be made something of. This is something that happens to every married man; he is always in danger of being made something of. Usually the process is a success. Just look at me, standing here in all my glory—by arrangement with some friends of mine called the Brothers Moss. You don't suppose I became the splendid figure I am today by my own efforts? No, Ladies and Gentlemen, I was made something of. May I now be perfectly serious as I ask you to raise your glasses to the bride and the groom. To the luckiest man in England, and his beautiful young wife.'

Specimen 3

'I am afraid I am not much of an orator. In fact I think the last speech I made in public was at my own wedding, which must have been about the time of the Boer War. Or was it the Crimean? One grows so forgetful as one grows older. However one thing no-one here today will ever forget is what a perfect picture Jean and Robert made today as they stood together in church. Mind you Jean was so late I began to wonder if we hadn't all turned up for nothing, but she made it in the end. Ah, well, it is the bride's privilege. She told me the reason she was so late was that she couldn't get her veil right. You all saw that she got it right in the end—and everything else as well. I dare say Robert didn't mind waiting for a girl who finally arrived looking such a picture. In any case I am sure they have such a long and happy future stretching before them that a few minutes here or there makes little difference. It doesn't matter so much, after all, if you are married at two o'clock or ten past two—so long as you are married to the right partner. And I have never been so sure of anything in my life as that these two have done just that—found the right partner. People always say at weddings something like "and I hope their married life will be as happy as my own." I'll add something to that. I'll say I hope their married life will be as happy as my wife has made my own. For it's a good wife that makes a good marriage—and that's just what Robert has managed to find. So I ask you to rise and lift your glasses as we drink a toast of long life and great happiness to the bride and groom.'

Notes

_____

_____

_____

_____

_____

_____

_____

_____

_____

_____

_____

_____

_____

_____

_____

_____

_____

_____

_____

_____

The bridegroom's reply

(and toast to the bridesmaids)

The bridegroom must respond to the toast to himself and his new wife, and propose a toast to the bridesmaids. He will therefore need to make four or five specific points in his speech, although again it should certainly not last for more than five minutes.

Firstly the bridegroom must express his and his wife's thanks for the good wishes of his new father-in-law. He should add here how happy he is to be joining his wife's family.

Secondly he may wish to thank his own parents for all they have done for him both over the years and during the preparations for the wedding. He may also want to extend particular public thanks to his best man.

Thirdly it is important to say what a pleasure it is to see so many friends gathered together, and to thank them all for their generous gifts. If a very old friend or close member of the family is unavoidably absent, regret can be added here.

Lastly the bridegroom must of course declare his admiration for the looks and efficiency of the bridesmaids, and announce his toast to them.

Specimen 1

'Ladies and Gentlemen—When I told my new father-in-law a few minutes ago that I felt nervous about making this speech, he said, "Don't be silly. Everyone *expects* a man to make a fool of himself on his wedding day. They'll be disappointed if you don't." And the last thing I want to do today is to disappoint you. I feel so happy that I want everyone else to be happy. Let me say too how delighted Jean and I are that you were all able to come to our wedding. Apart from anything else we would have felt pretty foolish sitting down here behind this enormous cake if there were no-one else to eat it! But we do sincerely thank you for coming, and for the beautiful presents you have given us. I have one or two personal thank-you's to make too. First to Jean's parents, who could not have been kinder to me, to the man who has stolen their daughter from them. Secondly to my best man. You wouldn't think, to see him sitting there idly supping champagne that he is one of the world's great organisers. Well, he is, and his organising ability has been of enormous help to me. And thirdly I must thank the bridesmaids. They all looked absolutely splendid, and if anyone could have stolen my new wife's thunder today, it would have been them. I ask you then to drink a toast to these delightful young women who supported Jean in her—I was going to say "ordeal"—in her big day. Ladies and Gentlemen—the bridesmaids.'

26

Specimen 2

'Ladies and Gentlemen—We are told that marriage is a lottery. If it is, then I must be the big winner. I really am the luckiest man in the world, to have found a wife like Jean and friends like you to come along and share my happiness. I have been lucky in other ways too. Lucky in my new parents-in-law. I don't like that phrase "in-law" much. Perhaps I could call them my "extra parents", for no-one could have been more kind to me than they have been. And no-one could be luckier in his best man than I have been—even if he did whisper in my ear just as Jean was coming up the aisle, "I do hope I haven't forgotten the ring." Jean has been lucky too—and I don't only mean in getting me for a husband! I mean in the support her charming bridesmaids have given her today. I think we should all raise our glasses to them, for looking so nice and acting so nicely! Ladies and Gentlemen—the bridesmaids.'

Specimen 3

'I woke up this morning and thought, "Bridegrooms are meant to be nervous, but there's nothing wrong with me." Then I put an entire packet of tea into the teapot, and poured boiling water into the empty tea caddy! Those days are over for ever! I am now a married man and life from now on will be much more organised. I see before me an endless stream of clean shirts and darned socks, for that, they tell me, is what married life is all about. Seriously, though, I do feel I'm the luckiest man alive to have wooed and won Jean. I like that phrase "wooed and won", it has an old-fashioned air about it. I suppose marriage is an old fashioned thing to some people, but I have a feeling it will be around for a long, long time. I hope so, anyway. I have been married (*looks at watch*) quite fifty minutes and I have no complaints at all! I want to say thank you on behalf of my wife to all of you for coming to our wedding and for being so absurdly generous in your presents. And I want to say thank you on my own behalf to Jean, for taking me on, to her parents for their tremendous kindness to me, and to my best man, who got me to the church on time! I have another duty, to propose the health of the bridesmaids. This is really more than a duty, it's a positive pleasure. I know they have been very helpful to Jean, not only today, but in those long weeks of preparation that brides go in for. And I know you will want me to thank them on your behalf for making my wedding such a pretty picture for the photographers. Ladies and Gentlemen—the bridesmaids.'

Notes

_____
_____
_____
_____
_____
_____
_____
_____
_____
_____
_____
_____
_____
_____
_____
_____
_____
_____
_____
_____

The best man's reply

(on behalf of the bridesmaids)

The best man's speech must be lighter in tone than those of the bride's father or the bridegroom. But this certainly does not make it any easier!

First and foremost the best man has to thank the bridegroom on behalf of the bridesmaids. He will then normally add his best wishes to the happy couple, and he may offer some thoughts on their future—of an amusing but never risqué nature. It is often useful to use an amusing anecdote or quotation at this point, to ensure the full attention of his audience.

At the end of his speech the best man will introduce and read any telegrams from absent friends. These should be vetted beforehand, and any that have a hint of vulgarity should be excluded from the public recital. It is also acceptable to group together several telegrams of simple good wishes, merely announcing the names of those who have sent them.

Specimen 1

'Ladies and Gentlemen—I am called the Best Man, but goodness knows why, for no-one pays much attention to a man in my position today. They all say, "Isn't the bride radiant?" and "Doesn't the bridegroom look dashing?" and "How pretty the bridesmaids are!" But you never hear anyone say, "What a fine figure of a man the Best Man is!" If they notice me at all they think I'm someone from the caterers. But enough of my troubles. I am standing up at this moment to speak for the bridesmaids, to say thank you on their behalf for the kind things Robert said about them. To tell you the truth I don't think he did them justice, but then that's understandable on a day like this. I'm surprised he even *noticed* that they were there at all, the way he's been looking at Jean. Never mind, I'm still a bachelor and my judgment is emotionally unclouded, and I think they're the finest looking set of bridesmaids I've ever seen. I can see that you all agree with me, so my job is done. On behalf of the bridesmaids, thank you very much indeed.'

Specimen 2

'I feel a little strange replying to the toast to the bridesmaids, because, as you can all see, I am not a bridesmaid. It is, however a very pleasant job, because I think we all feel that Robert was absolutely right in saying such nice things about them. I would like to thank him for saying nice things about me, too, though I must admit I do rather deserve them. I mean, where would a bridegroom be without his best man? The friend at hand when panic grips him on the very steps of the church. The reassuring voice in his ear when he is absolutely sure he has forgotten some vital detail in his honeymoon arrangements. The wise counsellor who knows just how everything should be done on the most important day in a man's life. I felt sure that Robert had picked me for this important job because he had weighed up my fine qualities and thought me ideal. And while we were sitting in church waiting for Jean to arrive I did ask him to confirm this. Do you know what he said? He said, "Oh, well, Eric is in Kuwait and I thought you might just about manage." Never mind, I forgive him. The only thing I find it hard to forgive him for is marrying this beautiful young woman, who must surely have preferred me had she known me a little better. Let me add my good wishes to this handsome couple, and let me say thank you most sincerely on behalf of the bridesmaids.'

Notes

_____

_____

_____

_____

_____

_____

_____

_____

_____

_____

_____

_____

_____

_____

_____

_____

_____

_____

_____

_____

_____

The bride's speech

There is really no need for the bride to say anything at all on her wedding day. Wedding etiquette allows no formal place for a speech from her.

However, the custom is growing for the bride to say just a very few words. The ideal place is immediately after her husband has responded to the toast to the two of them, but if he is proposing the toast to the bridesmaids this is difficult.

Sometimes the bride says her few words after her husband's response, and he then rises again to propose a separate toast to the bridesmaids. However this is not really satisfactory, and if the bride wishes to speak it is best that someone else is selected to propose the bridesmaids' health.

The pattern then is: proposal of the bride and groom's health followed by response by the groom, and a second response by the bride. Proposal of the bridesmaids' health by someone else, followed by response by the best man.

No-one is going to expect oratory from a bride on what is after all a day on which she must feel some nervous tension. Therefore no-one minds if she falters a little in her speech, or even sheds a tear or two.

Three or four sentences are quite enough for her to deliver publicly. Something like this is fine:

'Ladies and Gentlemen—I do not want to say very much. Just that this is the happiest day of my life, and to thank you all for coming to our wedding and being so generous with your gifts. I want to say a very special thank-you to Robert's parents, who have already made me feel I am their own daughter, and to my own parents for looking after me all my life, and then for recognising that Robert was the right man to hand me over to. Thank you.'

Notes

CHAPTER THREE

Useful Quotations

You have to be careful about putting quotations into a speech, for if you use more than two or three you can sound awfully pompous.

But quotations are useful in this way: they set you thinking, they start a train of thought which can make the thread of your speech.

And if you can find just one quotation that is especially apt to the particular circumstances of the wedding you are attending, by all means use it.

If you do use more than one quotation, make it clear that you have looked it up. Unless you are known as an erudite person, tell your audience where the quotations came from.

Say something like: 'I would pretend that these splendid literary quotations I am giving you came straight out of my memory. I *would* pretend—if Robert hadn't seen my poring over the "Oxford Dictionary of Quotations" two days ago.'

Or: 'Let me confess I had never heard that quotation until yesterday. Someone suggested it to me, and it seemed so apt I had to pass it on to you. Though this is such a highly intellectual gathering that I am sure you all knew it already!'

In other words, don't make a parade of learning. Throw your quotation in lightly, and develop it to suit the circumstances.

Here is an example of what I mean:

'Ladies and Gentlemen—As I rise to propose the health of the bride and groom, I am reminded of the words of William Congreve. (Reminded, I should say, by my wife, who looked it up last night.) Congreve said: "Though marriage makes man and wife one flesh, it leaves 'em two fools." Now just take a look at our two young fools. They

40

don't seem to mind their foolishness at all. They seem to be revelling in it! And when I look round at you distinguished people I can see quite a lot of old friends who have been two fools together for almost as long as have my wife and I. And they all seem perfectly happy in their foolishness. It is very pleasant, you know, to see through a thundering old cynic like Congreve. The most sensible thing a man can do is to find himself the right wife. . . .'

And so on.

Here is another example:

'There used to be a popular song which had this refrain, if I remember it properly: "Love makes the world go round." Any schoolboy will tell you that the world goes round because it can't stop spinning on its axis. But looking at Jean and Robert today, I think it is perfectly true to say that love makes *their* world go round. . . .'

One last example:

'You all know the old song: "Why am I always the bridesmaid, Never the blushing bride?" Well I feel like changing it a little and singing: "Why am I always the Best Man, Never the blushing bridegroom?" Because this is the third wedding at which I have been best man in eighteen months; if it goes on like this I shall lose my amateur status. Between you and me, I can tell you the real reason why I am on the shelf at twenty-two is that I've never met a girl like Jean. . . .'

There follows a number of useful quotations, grouped under the headings of 'Marriage', 'Love', and 'Various'.

Some of these quotations are not quite flattering about the institution of marriage—indeed some are positively cynical. However, these can be used to good effect provided of course that the speaker quotes them only to immediately deny the truth of their sentiments.

Marriage

For every marriage then is best in tune,
When that the wife is May, the husband's June.
—*Rowland Watkyns*.

Hanging and marriage, you know, go by destiny.
—*George Farquhar*.

Is not marriage an open question, when it is alleged from the beginning of the world, that such as are in the institution wish to get out, and such that are out wish to get in.
—*Ralph Waldo Emerson*.

Marriage is a wonderful institution, but who wants to live in an institution?
—*Groucho Marx*.

It won't be a stylish marriage.
I can't afford a carriage.

—*Harry Dacre*.

I would advise no man to marry, Sir,. . . . who is not likely to propagate understanding.

* * *

Marriage has many pains, but celibacy has no pleasures.

* * *

Marriages would in general be as happy, and often more so, if they were all made by the Lord Chancellor.

—*Dr Samuel Johnson.*

Marriage is nothing but a civil contract.

—*John Selden.*

Marriage is a sort of friendship recognised by the police.

* * *

No woman should marry a teetotaller.

* * *

To marry is to domesticate the Recording Angel. Once you are married there is nothing left for you, not even suicide, but to be good.

* * *

Times are changed with him who marries; there are no more by-path meadows, where you may innocently linger, but the road lies long and straight and dusty to the grave.

* * *

In marriage a man becomes slack and selfish, and undergoes a fatty degeneration of his moral being.

* * *

Marriage is like life in this: that it is a field of battle not a bed of roses.

*   *   *

Marriage is a step so grave and decisive that it attracts light-headed, variable men by its very awfulness.
—*Robert Louis Stevenson.*

It is a woman's business to get married as soon as possible, and a man's to keep unmarried as long as possible.

*   *   *

Marriage is popular because it combines the maximum of temptation with the maximum of opportunity.
—*George Bernard Shaw.*

Marriage the happiest bond of love might be,
If hands were only joined when hearts agree.
—*George Granville.*

Though marriage makes man and wife one flesh, it leaves 'em two fools.
—*William Congreve.*

For in what stupid age or nation,
Was marriage ever out of fashion?
—*Samuel Butler.*

When I said I would die a bachelor, I did not think I should live till I were married.

*   *   *

Let me not, to the marriage of true minds,
Admit impediments.

*   *   *

God, the best maker of all marriages,
Combine your hearts in one.

—*William Shakespeare.*

St Aldegonde had a taste for marriages and public executions.

—*Benjamin Disraeli.*

The reason why so few marriages are happy is because young ladies spend their time in making nets, not in making cages.

—*Jonathan Swift.*

One fool at least, in every married couple.

—*Henry Fielding.*

Love and marriage,
Love and marriage,
Go together like a horse and carriage.

—*Popular Song.*

Strange to say what delight we married people have to see these poor fools decoyed into our condition.

—*Samuel Pepys.*

Married in haste, we may repent at leisure.

—*William Congreve.*

I am to be married within these three days: married past redemption.

—*John Dryden.*

He is dreadfully married. He's the most married man I ever saw in my life.

—*Artemus Ward.*

Wen you're a married man, Samivel, you'll understand a good many things as you don't understand now; but vether it's worth while going through so much to learn so little, as the charity boy said ven he got to the end of the alphabet, is a matter o'taste.

—*Sam Weller*
(in Dickens' *Pickwick Papers*).

Advice to persons about to marry—don't.

—*Punch, 1845.*

Remember it's easy to marry a rich woman as a poor woman.

This I set down as a positive truth: a woman with fair opportunites and without a positive hump, may marry whom she likes.

—*William Makepeace Thackeray.*

For I'm not so old, and not so plain,
And I'm quite prepared to marry again.

—*W.S. Gilbert.*

A lady's imagination is very rapid; it jumps from admiration to love, from love to matrimony in a moment.

—*Jane Austen*

I wish you health—a little wealth
And a happy home with freedom.
And may you always have true friends
But never have cause to need them.

—*Anon*

The most popular after-dinner speech on record was made by a man dining with his wife alone in the privacy of their home, and it consisted of one sentence containing seven words of one syllable: "You leave them, dear, I'll do them."

—Anon

If men knew how women pass the time when they are alone, they'd never marry.

—O. Henry (W.S. Porter)

Wives are young men's mistresses; companions for middle age; and old men's nurses.

—Francis Bacon

When a man has married a wife, he finds out whether / Her knees and elbows are only glued together.

—William Blake

Marriage is an attempt to turn a night owl into a homing pigeon.

—Anon.

Chumps always make the best husbands. When you marry, Sally, grab a chump. Tap his forehead first, and if it rings solid, don't hesitate. All the unhappy marriages come from husbands having brains. What good are brains to a man? They only unsettle him.

—P.G. Wodehouse

Spring cleaning is a basic human experience. Faced in the right, it sets the seal on married love.

—Paul Jennings

I . . . chose my wife, as she did her wedding gown, not for a fine glossy surface, but such qualities as would wear well.

—Oliver Goldsmith

Love

Alas! The love of women! it is known
To be a lovely and a fearful thing.
—*Lord Bryon.*

Love makes the world go round.
—*Popular Song.*

The course of true love never did run smooth.
—*William Shakespeare.*

Can love be controlled by advice?
—*John Gay.*

Eternal joy, and everlasting love.
—*Thomas Otway.*

In the spring a young man's fancy, Lightly turns to thoughts of love.
  O hard, when love and duty clash!
—*Lord Tennyson.*

Did you ever heard of Captain Wattle?
He was all for love and a little for the bottle.
—*Charles Dibdin.*

I love a lassie.
—*Sir Harry Lauder.*

Having been in love with one princess or another almost all my life, and I hope I shall go on so, till I die, being firmly persuaded that if I ever do a mean action, it must be in some interval betwixt one passion and another.
—*Laurence Sterne.*

Let love be without dissimulation.
—*The Bible.*

Love is best.
—*Robert Browning.*

Love and murder will out.
                                        —*William Congreve.*

Love is more than gold or great riches.
                                        —*John Lydgate.*

Two souls with but a single thought,
Two hearts that beat as one.
                                        —*Maria Lovell*

Women are meant to be loved, not understood.
                                        —*Oscar Wilde*

And all for love, and nothing for reward.
                                        —*Edmund Spencer*

Of all forms of caution, caution in love is perhaps
the most fatal to true happiness.
                                        —*Bertrand Russell*

Oh! She was good as she was fair.
None—none on earth above her!
As pure in thought as angels are,
To know her was to love her.
                                        —*Samuel Rogers*

Various

All women become like their mothers. That is their tragedy. No man does. That's his.
—*Oscar Wilde.*

A mother's pride, a father's joy!
—*Sir Walter Scott.*

Blest is the bride on whom the sun doth shine.
—*Robert Herrick.*

Oh Woman, in our hours of ease,
Uncertain, coy and hard to please.
—*Sir Walter Scott.*

Fresh as a bridegroom.
—*William Shakespeare.*

Why am I always the bridesmaid,
Never the blushing bride?
—*Old Song.*

A happy bridesmaid makes a happy bride.
—*Lord Tennyson.*

I am no orator as Brutus is; but you know me all a plain, blunt man.
—*William Shakespeare.*

Be sure to leave other men their turns to speak.
—*Francis Bacon.*

I have always thought that every woman should marry and no man.
—*Benjamin Disraeli.*

A woman is only a woman, but a cigar is a good smoke.
—*Rudyard Kipling.*

I for one venerate a petticoat.

—*Lord Byron.*

Woman will be the last thing civilised by man.
—*George Meredith.*

An honest man's the noblest work of God.
—*Alexander Pope.*

A wise man makes more opportunities than he finds.

—*Francis Bacon.*

Apologise to a man if you're wrong, but to a woman even if you're right.

—*Anon*

An after dinner speaker is a man who rises to the occasion and then stands too long.

—*Anon*

In public speaking, if you don't strike oil in five minutes, stop boring.

—*Anon*

Blessed is the man who having nothing to say, abstains from giving us wordy evidence of the fact.

—*George Eliot*

They conquer who think they can.

—*John Dryden*

Everything comes to him that hustles while he waits.

—*Thomas A. Edison*

Often when we ask for advice we want approval.

—*Anon*

An old man gives good advice in order to console himself for no longer being in a condition to set a bad example.

—*La Rochefoucauld*

Men are like fish; neither would get into trouble if they kept their mouths shut.

—*Anon*

CHAPTER FOUR

Comic Stories

There was a time when it was considered not quite proper to tell a joke or a funny story in the course of a wedding speech. Times change, and at all but the most formal weddings, a humorous anecdote is quite acceptable.

But the story you tell must be the kind you could tell the vicar, or your elderly maiden aunt.

This is one time when no hint of the blue or the risqué can be allowed to creep in, for fear of embarrassing the bride and groom.

So:

No stories about honeymoons, wedding nights, commercial travellers having amorous adventures are allowable.

You can include a quiet joke about vicars—especially if the one who officiated attends the reception—and mild jokes about nagging wives and lazy husband are all right, so long as you put in a disclaimer making it clear you are not talking about the happy couple!

There is one rule you should follow: one joke, and make it a short one. There is nothing more boring than the guest who fancies himself as a comedian and tells a string of long stories.

If you can, don't just tell your joke. Try to make it relevant to your speech in some way. Say something like: 'How nice it is to see the vicar here today. He was telling me just after the ceremony about a clerical friend of his who . . .' and then launch into your story.

Or: 'This splendid turn-out reminds me of another wedding I attended a few weeks ago. I heard a very good story there, and since I am not above a little light larceny, I shall tell it to you as my own. . . .'

Or: 'What excellent champagne this is, by the way. It makes me think of a friend of mine who enjoyed champagne very much. One day he drank a little too much of the stuff and . . .'

Here are a few stories you may find useful:

A small boy was fishing in a canal one Sunday morning, when the vicar passed him on his way to church. 'Don't you know it is sinful to fish on the Sabbath?' he asked. 'I'm not fishing,' said the boy. 'I'm teaching a worm to swim.'

* * *

A diplomat was seated at an important banquet next to an important visitor from China. He realised that it would be rude to say nothing, but what on earth could one say to a Chinese? The soup arrived, and desperately the diplomat smiled and said 'Likee soupee?' The Chinese nodded, and that was the extent of their conversation throughout the meal. After the coffee the visitor was called upon to speak. He rose and made an excellent speech in faultless English, without a trace of an accent. Then he sat down and said to the diplomat: 'Likee speechee?'

Two farm hands were talking about politics. 'With this system I've been reading about,' said George, 'it's share and share alike.' William got the idea. 'You mean,' he said, 'that if you win £10,000 on the pools you'll give me half?' George nodded. 'And if you live in a big house and I have to sleep in the barn, you'll let me have half the house?' George nodded. 'And if you've got a pig and I haven't, you'll let me have half the pig?' George thought a bit. 'No,' he said, 'I've *got* a pig.'

*　　*　　*

The judge and the bishop were arguing about who had the most power. Said the bishop, 'It's true you can say to a man "You be hanged." But I can go farther. I can say "You be damned."' 'That may be true,' said the judge. 'But if I say to a man "You be hanged", he *is* hanged.'

*　　*　　*

The policeman was giving evidence in a case of drunken driving. 'The defendant,' he said, 'was as drunk as a judge . . .' The judge broke in: 'Surely you mean as drunk as a lord?' Said the policeman: 'Yes, my lord.'

*　　*　　*

The governor of Dartmoor was going round his jail when he saw a new prisoner dictating a letter to a prison officer. 'What is this man in for and why are you taking down his letter?' the governor asked the officer. 'He's in for forgery, sir, and I am taking this letter because he can't write.' The governor was astonished. 'If you can't write,' he asked the prisoner, 'how on earth were you convicted for forgery?' Said the prisoner: 'Rotten lawyer.'

The wife of a bus conductor was angry with him because every time he came home after working a late shift he woke both her and the children. Next night he tried really hard. He took off his shoes at the door and crept silently up the stairs. When he got to the top he forgot himself and shouted 'Fares, please!'

* * *

A woman who was delighted with the effect some patent medicine was having on her, wrote to tell the makers. 'Since taking your tablets I am a different woman,' she wrote. 'My husband is delighted.'

* * *

Two psychologists were watching a gang of navvies at work. 'Look,' said one, 'while the rest of them push their wheelbarrows, one pulls his. Do you suppose there is some deep-rooted explanation of this?' His friend thought. 'Let us talk to the fellow,' he said. So they asked the navvy if he knew why he pulled his barrow instead of pushing it. 'Blimey,' said the navvy. 'I'ates the sight of the thing.'

* * *

A party of American advertising men visiting Britain were allowed to watch Convocation at work. When the session broke up one of them managed to buttonhole the Archbishop of Canterbury. He was talking to him for some time. At lunch the bishops asked their leader what it was all about. 'He offered to give the Church several million dollars if I would authorise a small change in the wording of the Lord's Prayer,' said the Archbishop. 'We could certainly make good use of the money,' one bishop put in. 'What exactly did he want you to do?' 'Well,' said the Archbishop, 'all he wanted was to change "Give us this day our daily bread" to "Give us this day our daily Brekkywek's Cornflakes".'

*   *   *

The bishop served wine to all his dinner guests save one, an elderly spinster on his right. 'Could I have a little wine?' she ventured finally. 'My dear lady,' said the bishop. 'I am so sorry. I thought you were the secretary of the Temperance League.' The old lady corrected him. 'The Purity League,' she said. 'Of course, of course,' said the bishop. 'I knew there was something you didn't do.'

*   *   *

A certain peer had a nightmare. He dreamed he was addressing the House of Lords in a speech that was the most boring and interminable you could imagine. Then he woke up to find he *was* addressing the House of Lords.

*   *   *

An old gardener was worried about an operation his doctor said was necessary. 'Are you quite sure, sir, as it will be all right afterwards, like? Will I be able to dig the ground?' 'Perfectly,' said the doctor. 'Will I be able to get down on me knees to thin out the little seedlings?' 'Certainly,' said the doctor. 'And when it's all over and I'm out of the hospital, will I be able to grow orchids?' 'Of course,' said the doctor. The gardener scratched his head. 'That's very peculiar,' he said, ''cos I never have been able to grow 'em before.'

* * *

In the weeks before her wedding a young bride was terribly anxious in case she made some mistake at the ceremony. The vicar reassured her several times, pointing out that the service was quite simple. 'All you have to remember,' he said, 'is that when you enter the church you walk up the AISLE. The groom and best man will be waiting before the ALTAR. Then I shall ask the congregation to sing a HYMN and we shall get on with the ceremony. Just remember the order in which those things happen and you can't go wrong.' On the big day the bridegroom waited nervously for his bride to appear. When she arrived and stood alongside him, he heard her quietly repeating to herself 'Aisle, altar, hymn, aisle, altar, hymn.' Or, as it seemed to him, 'I'll alter him!'

* * *

A big game hunter met a leopard. 'What are you looking for?' asked the leopard. 'A leopard-skin coat,' said the hunter, raising his gun, 'and what are *you* after?' The leopard replied: 'Breakfast, and let's not be hasty about this. Come round to my den and I may be able to help you.' The hunter put down his gun and went with the leopard to his den. A little later the leopard walked out alone, having had a fine breakfast. And the hunter was wrapped in a beautiful leopardskin coat.

*　　*　　*

'I'm afraid we'll overlook some insignificant little detail,' said the girl who was to be married in a week, as she and her mother were working through the arrangements. 'Don't worry,' said the mother, 'I'll see he gets there.'

*　　*　　*

As their taxi drove up to the railway station the new bride turned to her new husband and whispered, 'Darling, I don't want the porters to guess we're newlyweds. I want them to think we've been married for years.' The groom looked a bit dubious. 'Are you *sure* you can manage both suitcases, darling?' he asked.

*　　*　　*

They had been married a year, and one day she shyly confessed to him that she had bought ten new dresses. 'Ten!' he exploded. 'What could any wife want with ten new dresses?' She smiled at him sweetly. 'Ten new hats?' she ventured.

*　　*　　*

Henry Ford was making a tour of his plant. He stopped by one grizzled workman. 'How long have you been working for me?' he asked. 'Thirty-five years,' said the man proudly, 'and in all that time I have made just one small mistake.' Ford shook his hand. 'But from today,' he said, 'I want you to be more careful.'

*　　*　　*

An Australian sheep farmer ordered a Rolls-Royce limousine. After a few months Rolls sent their Australian representative along to see how he was making out with the car. 'Best I ever had,' said the farmer, 'and what I like best is that glass division between the back seats and the front ones.' The Rolls man was puzzled. 'Why, that's not so special,' he said. 'No?' the farmer answered. 'First car I've had where the sheep didn't lick the back of my neck on the way to market.'

*　　*　　*

Did you hear about the man who was teaching his girl to play golf? She hit one ball pretty well, and he went off to report the lie of it. 'Good heavens!' he called back, 'it's a dead stymie.' She was most distressed. 'Did I hit it?' she asked.

*　　*　　*

'You are the defendant, and you plead not guilty to stealing these chickens?' said the magistrate. 'I plead not guilty,' said the man in the dock, 'but I'm not the defendant. I'm only the man who stole the chickens.'

*　　*　　*

'Why do they call this hotel The Palms?' said one guest to another. 'I can't see a single palm tree.' Said the second guest: 'Just watch the waiters on the day you go home.'

*　*　*

A young man was trying to explain the mysteries of horse-racing to a young woman. 'If you back a horse for a pound at five to one, you win five pounds. If you back it at ten to one, you get ten pounds. And if you back it at twenty to one, you get twenty pounds.' She answered sweetly: 'And what happens if I back it at exactly one o'clock?'

*　*　*

A noble lord loved to organise a cricket week at his stately home. But for one important match they were missing an umpire, so the first footman was called in to do the job. While he was batting the noble lord was rapped smartly on the pad, and the bowler yelled 'Owzat?' Said the umpire-footman: 'His lordship is not at home.' His employer stared at him. 'What are you talking about?' he demanded. 'I mean,' said the footman, 'that you're out.'

*　*　*

A man walked into a poultry shop and asked for a brace of pheasants. 'Out of season,' said the poulterer. 'A hare, then?' asked the man. 'No,' said the shopkeeper, 'but how about a nice pork pie?' The man thought. 'No,' he said, 'you see I can't actually say I've *shot* a pork pie, can I?'

*   *   *

A guest who could not manage to get to the church in time, turned up at the reception and began searching around for the groom, whom he had not met. He saw one elegant young man in morning dress and asked him: 'Are you the bride-groom?' The young man shook his head and said sadly: 'I was eliminated in the semi-finals.'

*   *   *

A man was spending the week-end with friends. On Sunday morning he rose early, went downstairs and found only the six-year-old son of the house up. The boy produced a hammer and a bag of six-inch nails and started to hammer them into a beautiful antique table. 'Daddy lets me do this,' said the lad, when the guest tried to stop him. Just then the boy's father came in and con-firmed the little game was permitted. 'But don't you find it rather expensive?' asked the guest. 'No,' said the father, 'we get the nails wholesale.'

*   *   *

Some years ago an international conference took place, at which the British and Russian ambassadors were both delegates. Relaxing over coffee one evening these two gentlemen decided to settle a bet by holding a race. The story got out, and when the time came for the race to be run there was quite an audience of members of the Press. The Times reported the event in the following way:

'A race took place yesterday between the British and Russian Ambassadors. The British Ambassador won.'

Izvestia told the story slightly differently:

'A race took place between Ambassadors. The Russian Ambassador came second. The British Ambassador was last but one.'

*   *   *

A psychiatrist opened the door to receive his next patient, and saw to his surprise that she was carrying a live duck under her arm. Naturally, being a psychiatrist of some considerable experience, he refrained from any comment. Instead he offered the lady a seat and asked how he could help her.

'Oh no doctor,' she replied, 'it's not me who needs help, it's my husband. I've brought him in because he thinks he's a duck.'

*   *   *

One day in ancient Rome, the Emperor was entertaining his guests at the Coliseum where Christians were being thrown to the lions.

He was not amused however, when one of the Christians seemed to whisper in the attacking lion's ear, at which the great roaring beast turned tail and slunk off. The Christian did the same thing as each lion leapt up to him, with the same instant and astonishing effect.

The Emperor was furious, but also intrigued. He had the Christian brought before him and promised to spare his life if he would reveal his secret power over the lions.

'I have no special magic Your Highness,' the Christian replied. 'I simply tell them that they will of course have to make a speech to the assembled crowd after they have finished their dinner.'

*　　*　　*

A widowed woman has kept a parrot for many years but eventually he dies and hoping to replace her long-time companion she goes to the pet shop to buy another.

'Well, we do have a parrot,' the man says, 'but I couldn't sell him to you—he's such an awful swearer.'

'That's alright,' says the widow, 'I'm used to parrots. I'll soon stop him swearing.'

So she takes the parrot home and puts him in his cage, whereupon he lets out such a string of abusive language that the widow is furious.

'Right, my lad, 'she says,' I'll soon stop your swearing.' And she takes him from the cage, puts him in the fridge and closes the door. So there the parrot is standing on the shelf shivering when he notices a chicken on the shelf below, plucked, trussed and lying on a plate with its legs in the air.

'Good Lord,' exclaims the parrot. 'What on earth did you say to the old cow?'

*　　*　　*

Two elderly gentlemen were sitting in their club, engaged in desultory conversation and gazing rather vacantly out of the window. Suddenly a very pretty girl, wearing a very tight skirt, came into view and walked quickly past the window. Immediately there followed a young man, walking just a little bit faster than the girl and gaining steadily on her. The first old man perked up and said, 'Do you remember how we used to chase the pretty girls down the street?' The second old fellow hardly stirred and replied wearily; 'Yes, I do remember how we used to chase them, but I can't for the life of me remember why.''

*　　*　　*

A Yorkshireman visits a stonemason to chose a headstone for his dead wife.

'Now, Bert,' he says. 'I want something really tasteful for Mabel. She was a God-fearing woman so let's be having your best effort.'

'Certainly Sam,' says the stonemason. 'This is our best headstone and on it you could have written 'Mabel Higginbottom—Faithful Wife and Mother' followed by a nice inscription.

'Yes—but what inscription?'

'Well let's go into the office and have a look at the catalogue.'

They go into the stonemason's office and the Yorkshireman looks through the list of inscriptions.

'This is it,' he says excitedly. 'Very nice—"She was Thine". Mabel was a God-fearing woman. She would have liked that.'

'Alright,' says the stonemason. 'We'll have "Mabel Higginbottom—Faithful Wife and Mother—She was Thine". Come back next week and Sid will have inscribed the headstone and it will be ready.'

Next week the Yorkshireman goes back to the stonemason's.

'Now then, Bert—is our Mabel's headstone ready?'

'Yes it is, Sam. Come round the back and have a look.'

They go round to the back of the yard and the Yorkshireman looks at the headstone.

'But what's this?' he says, '"Mabel Higginbottom—Faithful Wife and Mother—She was Thin! She was Thin?"'

The stonemason looks at the headstone. 'Oh dear, Sid has left out the E.' He turns round and calls out. 'Here, Sid. You've missed out an E on this inscription." He turns back to the Yorkshireman.

'Never mind, Sam. Come back next week and Sid will have done it.'

The following week the Yorkshireman returns

to the stonemason's.

'Well now, Bert. Is our Mabel's headstone ready?''

'It is that. Sid has put the E on and it's done. Come and have a look.'

They go round to the back of the yard and the Yorkshireman reads the inscription.

'"Mabel Higginbottom—Faithful Wife and Mother—Eeh She was Thin"!'

*　　*　　*

A mother and son go into a police station.

'I want to report a missing person.'

'Certainly madam. We'll just have to take a description.' The desk sergeant reaches down the register. 'Now what does the missing person look like?'

'Well he's about six foot tall, blond, blue eyed, about twenty eight years old. . . . . . .'

At that moment the child breaks in. 'But Mum, that doesn't sound anything like my Dad.'

'Shut up—we don't want him back.'

*　　*　　*

A couple visit a Chinese restaurant and the Chinese waiter comes to the table to take their order.

'What you rike to eat?' he asks.

They order a complete meal which duly arrives. They eat their way through the first two courses which are reasonable and then they start on the chicken dish. This is so unpalatable that the man calls over the waiter.

'Excuse me,' he says, 'but this chicken is rubbery.'

'Oh, thank you very much. Grad you like it.'

*　　*　　*

67

A man with a terrible stutter goes into a book-makers shop.

'I've b. . . . b. . . . b. . . . backed a f. . . . f. . . . f. . . . four t. . . . t. . . . t. . . . . t. . . . t. . . . .'

The bookmaker tries to help him out. 'Alright—you've backed a four to one winner. How much was the stake?'

'It was a f. . . . f. . . . . f. . . . . f. . . . . f. . . . . f. . . . .'

At this point the bookmaker completely loses patience. 'A five pound stake?' He thrusts a twenty pound note into the stutterer's hand.

'Here—take this and get out. I can't wait around all day while you try to spill it out.'

The stutterer leaves the shop and stands outside on the pavement scratching his head and looking at the twenty pound note in his hand.

At that moment a friend passes. 'Hello there—had a win?'

The stutterer shakes his head. 'N. . . . n. . . . n. . . . no. I just t. . . . t. . . t. . . tried to t. . . . t. . . t. . . tell him I've b. . . b. . . b. . . b. . . . backed a f. . . . f. . . . f. . . . four t. . . . t. . . . t. . . . . ton truck into his Rolls Royce.'

*   *   *

A most inexperienced speaker found himself having to propose the first toast at a large gathering of distinguished ladies and gentlemen. At last the meal was drawing to a close and he knew that he must prepare himself for the inevitable ordeal. The toastmaster came up behind him and whispered; 'Are you ready to speak now sir, or shall I let the guests go on enjoying themselves for a little longer?'

*   *   *

Two polar bears, father and son, are sitting on an ice flow talking.

'Dad,' says one, 'am I really a polar bear?'

'Of course you are, son. I'm a polar bear, your mother's a polar bear, all your brothers and sisters are polar bears—of course you're a polar bear.'

Two days later the little polar bear is sitting with his grandfather on the ice cap.

'Grandad,' says the little one, 'am I really a polar bear?'

'Of course you are son. I'm a polar bear, your granny's a polar bear, all your family are polar bears. Of course you're a polar bear.' The very next day the little polar bear is sitting on an ice flow with his mother.

'Mum,' he says, 'am I really a polar bear?'

'Of course you are, son. I'm a polar bear, your father's a polar bear—what on earth makes you think that you might not be a polar bear?'

'Well, Mum—it's just that I always feel so dreadfully cold.'

*   *   *

There were two elderly sisters who attended their local church every Sunday morning with absolute regularity. The vicar was a truly good and holy man, but he had one fault—that his sermons were interminably long. One Sunday he had gone on, and on, for even longer than was usual. The older of the two sisters, who was very deaf, turned to the other and said, 'Has he not finished yet?' To which the younger replied, loud and clear, 'Yes, he's finished alright, but he can't seem to stop.'

*   *   *

A man goes to the doctor's suffering with terrible earache. But when he gets there instead of his usual doctor he finds an Indian locum.

'I am Dr Singh,' he says. 'What can I do to help?'

'Well, it's this earache again. I usually get drops from the doctor and they do the trick.'

'Earache? Let me see.' And he takes a torch-like instrument and looks down the man's ear. 'Ah, yes. I have a cure for this. You go home and boil the kettle. You make a pot of tea. You then dry the tea leaves and stick them in your ear. After a week you come back to see me.'

So the man goes home and does as the doctor told him then after a week comes back again.

'Ah, yes—the earache,' the doctor says. 'Let me have a look.' And again he sticks the torch-like instrument in the man's ear.

He is quiet for a very long time so eventually the man asks, 'Can you see anything, doctor?'

The doctor sighs, 'Yes—you are going on a long journey. . . . . '

* * *

Jokes of the more risky variety

Here is a wedding day weather forecast—Two warm fronts are approaching, followed by a little sun later.

* * *

A couple were discussing their wedding plans. 'Where would you like to go for the honeymoon?' the groom asked. The bride gazed at him adoringly, 'Darling, with you I'd go anywhere. But since you are asking me, I'd like to go somewhere warm, somewhere different and somewhere that I've never been before.' So he took her into the kitchen.

* * *

A newly married couple went to Eastbourne for their honeymoon where the hotel was full of rather elderly ladies. When the young couple arrived, the bride, feeling rather nervous and self-conscious, whispered to her husband, 'Don't tell them that we're on our honeymoon, I don't want anyone to know we're just married.'

Next morning the young couple came down to breakfast to be greeted by frowns and disapproving looks. 'I wonder why they're all looking at us so disapprovingly,' whispered the blushing bride. 'Well you told me you didn't want them to know we're honeymooners,' said her husband. 'So, I told them we're not married.'

* * *

Donald Duck gets married and goes away on honeymoon. When the happy couple arrive at the hotel they waddle straight upstairs and prepare to get ready for bed. 'I hope you've brought some condoms,' murmurs the blushing bride. 'You know what they say about safe sex.' 'Good heavens,' says Donald, 'I haven't got any. I'd better go downstairs and see if I can buy some.' He waddles downstairs and asks the hall porter who opens the hotel shop and gets some for him. 'Shall I put them on your bill, sir,' he asks as he hands the condoms to Donald. 'Certainly not,' says Donald. 'What do you think I am—some kind of pervert?'

*　　*　　*

Mother and daughter are talking just prior to the daughter's wedding. The daughter asks, 'But mum, will he still respect me after we are married?' The mother answers, 'That's up to you. But take my advice and never let him see you totally naked. I've never let your father see me without something on, and he has respected me for over thirty years.'

About six months after the wedding, the son-in-law speaks to the mother. 'Is there something wrong with your Mary, mum?' he asks. 'What do you mean—something wrong?' 'Well we've been married now for six months and she hasn't taken her hat off yet.'

*　　*　　*

A pair of newly weds arrive in the bridal suite very anxious to get their clothes off. She strips naked and drops her clothes on the floor. He strips off, puts all her clothes on, and she has never seen him since.

*　　*　　*

A young boy asks his father. 'Dad, did I go on honeymoon with you and my mother?' The father replies, 'Well son, you went with me, and came back with your mother.'

* * *

Two middle-aged ladies were talking about marriage. 'Well, my dear,' said one. 'I haven't seen my husband for twenty-five years. He just went out to get a cabbage and never came back.' 'Good Lord,' exclaimed the other. 'What on earth did you do?' 'Oh, I just opened a tin of peas.'

* * *

Husband and wife are lying in bed when there's a sudden noise downstairs. 'Just go downstairs and see what it is,' the wife says. 'It might be a burglar.' 'Nah,' says the husband, turning over. 'I'm staying here where it's safe and warm.' 'Hmm—I thought you were brave when you married me.' 'So did all my mates.'

* * *

Two men were having a discussion about families and relations, and one man confessed that he had twenty three brothers and sisters.

'Good Lord!' exclaimed the other. 'That's an awful lot—how is it that you have so many?'

'Well I always thought it was because of my mother's deafness.'

'Why is that?'

'Well at night in bed, just before they turned out the lights, we used to hear my father say, "Well are you going to go to sleep or what?" and mother always used to reply, "What?".'

* * *

It is the company's dinner and dance. At the head table are the managing director, the finance manager, the sales manager and their wives. The meal is over, the speeches have been made and the dancing commences. Just then a beautiful blonde gets up, approaches the head table and asks the sales manager to dance. And off they go while the sales manager's wife sits there seething. When he gets back to the table the wife asks icely, 'And WHO was that?'

'Oh, that was Miss Jones—my mistress.'

'Your mistress!' she exclaims. 'Well that's it—I want a divorce.'

The sales manager sighs. 'All right, dear—but I hope you realise that we'll have to sell the house, the kids will have to boarding school, your American Express Gold Card will have to go back and your six foreign holidays a year will have to be cancelled.'

The wife sits there thinking this over when a beautiful red head gets up, walks to the head table and asks the managing director to dance.

'And who's the red head?' the sales manager's wife asks.

'Oh, that's Miss Smith—the managing director's mistress.

The sales manager's wife thinks for a moment then sniffs, ''Hmmm—she's not as nice as ours.'

⁂   ⁂   ⁂

An eighty-six-year-old man is talking to his barber. 'Give me a good trim, Bert. I'm getting married in the morning.' 'Fancy,' the barber exclaims, 'Wanting to get married at your age!' 'I don't want to—I've got to!'

⁂   ⁂   ⁂

A woman goes to the dentist for a check-up. She is very nervous. She hates dentists and hasn't been for some time. So she fusses about taking her coat off and hanging it up, looking in her handbag for a tissue. All the time the dentist is waiting patiently. 'Oh, I'm sorry to be such a silly,' she says. 'But I really hate going to the dentists. I'd rather do anything else.' Eventually she sits in the dentist's chair, but she won't lie back and is still fiddling with her handbag. 'Oh, I'm sorry to be so nervous— but I really do hate going to the dentist's—I'd rather have a baby than have my teeth pulled out.' 'Well make up your mind what you're going to do,' the dentist replies stoically. 'I want to adjust the seat.'

*　　*　　*

Your Own Jokes

_____

_____

_____

_____

_____

_____

_____

_____

_____

_____

_____

_____

_____

_____

_____

_____

_____

_____

_____

_____

_____

CHAPTER FIVE

Wedding Telegrams

It often happens that for one reason or another we cannot attend a wedding. The form here is write expressing regret to the bride's parents and to send a present. An informal note in addition to either the bride or groom, if either is a close friend, is permissible.

And on the day you may care to send a Greetings Telegram to wherever the reception is being held.

Basically the telegram must carry your good wishes, but these need not be expressed in too formal terms. The reading out of wittily composed telegrams can add gaiety to a wedding reception. Usually the best man or the bride's father will read them out.

Here are a few examples you may be able to use. Do not copy them exactly, but adapt them to the individual circumstances.

CONGRATULATIONS IN ADVANCE ON YOUR GOLDEN WEDDING ANNIVERSARY ON (*here insert date exactly 50 years from the wedding day*).

DELIGHTED YOU HAVE DECIDED TO JOIN THE REST OF US. CERTAIN YOU WILL LIVE HAPPILY EVER AFTER.

KNOW HOW HAPPY YOU WILL BE. REGRET ENORMOUSLY MISSING YOUR WEDDING. PLEASE SAVE SLICE OF CAKE PLUS BOTTLE OF CHAMPAGNE FOR ME.

COULD NOT HAVE HAPPENED TO NICER COUPLE. BEST WISHES TO ROBERT AND HIS YOUNG DUTCH.

BEST WISHES TO THE NEWLYWEDS FROM THE OLD-WEDS.

CONGRATULATIONS TO THE PRETTIEST BRIDE IN BRITAIN AND THE MAN WHO WAS LUCKY ENOUGH TO GET HER.

WISH I COULD BE WITH YOU TO SHARE YOUR HAPPINESS. KNOW THERE WOULD BE PLENTY TO GO ROUND.

WELL DONE ROBERT. MAY EVEN TAKE THE PLUNGE MYSELF NOW IF I CAN FIND A GIRL LIKE JEAN.

TO THE HAPPIEST COUPLE IN THE COUNTRY—MR AND MRS ROBERT SMITH.

Of course you would only send this type of telegram to people you knew well. To mere acquaintances something like this would do:

SINCERE WISHES ON YOUR WEDDING DAY.

Or:

CONGRATULATIONS ON YOUR WEDDING.

In the rare cases where a member of the immediate family of either bride or groom cannot be present, through illness or some unavoidable commitment, the telegram should be couched in warm terms.
Something like this perhaps:

SO HAPPY TO WELCOME MY NEW BROTHER ROBERT INTO THE FAMILY. DELIGHTED THAT MY SISTER JEAN HAS BEEN ABLE TO JOIN HIS. ALL MY LOVE. . . .

CHAPTER SIX

Wedding Etiquette

It is not within the scope of this book to deal exhaustively with wedding etiquette, but I find there is a surprisingly ignorance of this simple subject.

Most of the wedding arrangements are made by the bride's mother and father. It is their duty to see that the wedding invitations are sent out, after discussion with the groom and his family over whom they shall invite.

But before the formal cards go out, close friends and relatives *must* be informed in personal letters. Something quite simple: 'You will be glad to hear that Jean and Robert's wedding has been arranged for March 25. We shall, of course, be sending you a formal invitation later, but we felt sure you would be delighted to have the news as soon as possible.'

Later, when invitation cards are sent out, they must be composed in the third person, like this:

Mr and Mrs James Wedgwood request the pleasure of . . . . . .'s company at the marriage of their daughter Jean with Mr Robert Arbuthnot at St George's, Hanover Square on Wednesday March 25, at 2.15 p.m. and afterwards at a reception at the Dorchester Hotel.

Strictly speaking the reply to this invitation, which should be sent as soon as possible, should be in the third person too:

Mr Arthur Wickstead-Greene thanks Mr and Mrs Wedgwood for their kind invitation to the wedding of their daughter Jean. He will be delighted to attend.

It is still best to use this form when you do not know the parents well. But if they are well known to you, the third person these days is considered unnecessarily 'grand', and even a little silly.

But if you choose the first person, your letter should still be brief, and certainly not chatty. It should say simply:

Thank you for your kind invitation to Jean's wedding. I shall be delighted to attend.

If you cannot attend, your reply should be similarly brief. No-one wants to know in great detail why you can't make it. Simply say that because you are forced to be in another part of the country, or because you are not well enough, you will not be able to attend.

In any case, you must answer a wedding invitation—indeed any invitation—within three days.

If you are invited to a wedding, you should send a present, though of course one present will suffice for a husband and wife or a family who are all attending.

If you are unsure about what to give, simply write to the bride and ask her what she would like. Many girls have a list of 'most-wanted' gifts which include both expensive and inexpensive items.

The bride should write to thank all the people who have sent presents, but if the number is very large, there is no reason why her mother and her sisters should not write thank-you letters on her behalf.

Very early on in the planning the best man and bridesmaids should be chosen. For a small register office affair some couples do without both, though a best man is useful at any type of ceremony.

He should be unmarried and a good friend of the groom, and he ought to be a cheerful fellow who will not panic if some slight hitch occurs. It is his job to take all the worries from the groom's shoulders. He helps the groom to dress; he looks after the ring and all the documents for the groom.

The bridesmaids were at one time always chosen from the unmarried sisters of both families, but it is now quite normal for unmarried friends of the bride to do this job. A chief bridesmaid should be appointed; she will normally be the oldest unmarried sister of the bride. It is her job not only to supervise the other bridesmaids, but to act as chief helper to the bride. She is the bride's 'best man' if you like.

The bridegroom normally gives each bridesmaid a small present—some small article of jewellery is usual—and this is often worn at the ceremony.

Another early decision concerns what the bride shall wear. If the bride is to wear a traditional white wedding dress, then the groom and all male guests *should* wear morning dress. But at a great many white weddings the groom wears an ordinary lounge suit, and the other male guests do the same. This is perfectly acceptable, so long as the groom's suit is in some dark colour—not brown please.

Again, in earlier times the groom always wore a hat. But in these informal times many go bare-headed, and no-one minds.

The traditional white wedding is essentially a church affair and would look out of place at a register office ceremony. Here the bride may wear whatever she pleases. A suit or an afternoon dress are the usual choices. And the bride who marries in church but does not want a white wedding would wear the same sort of thing.

At a church ceremony guests should take their places about fifteen minutes before the given time. Normally the groom and best man will have appointed ushers, young men, either friends or family, who will help to seat the congregation. Custom dictates that the bride's followers sit on the left of the aisle, the bridegroom's on the right.

While the church is filling up, the bridegroom enters with his best man and stands at the chancel barrier to await his bride. She enters last, on the arm of her father, followed by her bridesmaids.

At the barrier she meets her bridegroom for the first time that day and stands on his left. Her father stands to the left too, a little to the rear. The best man stands on the bridegroom's right, also a little to the rear. The chief bridesmaid stands behind the bride, but farther back than her father. The other bridesmaids are ranged behind her.

The minister conducts the ceremony, and when the point is reached for the ring to be placed on the third finger of the bride's left hand, the best man hands the ring to the groom. (Sometimes the ring is previously handed to the priest, in which case he gives it to the groom at the appropriate moment.)

The bride hands her bouquet, if she has one, to her chief bridesmaid, at this stage. (The chief bridesmaid simply moves forward a pace or two, takes the bouquet, and returns to her place.)

After the ceremony the bride and groom with their near relatives and perhaps close friends, go to the vestry to sign the register. The bride signs her maiden name for the last time. She takes the bridegroom's left arm and they leave the church for home, or wherever the reception is to be held.

They take the first car, and no-one shares it with them. If there are further official cars, the second takes the bride's mother and the bridegroom's father, followed by the bridegroom's mother and the bride's father. Next go the bridesmaids and then the other guests.

The best man waits until everyone else has been found a place.

At the reception the bride's parents first receive the guests, who then congratulate the bride and groom and inspect the presents, if they are laid out.

(A register office ceremony is much less formal, and the order of leaving for the reception is not important. Even so the bride and groom must be allowed to travel on their own.)

The traditional wedding breakfast—which is in fact a luncheon—has been dying out in recent years. What has replaced it is the buffet reception in which light refreshments and drinks are handed round.

But if a formal meal is eaten, the bride and groom sit at the centre of the top table, the bride on her husband's left. On her left sits her father, on his left her mother-in-law. On the bridegroom's right sits his mother-in-law on her right his father.

The cake is customarily placed on the top table, but until the moment of cutting it should not be directly in front of the newlyweds. For if it is a tall cake it could obscure them from the sight of some guests.

The toasts come about halfway through the reception. It is important to see that everyone has a charged glass when they are made. There is nothing worse than seeing a guest raise an empty glass, and *mime* drinking a health.

The wedding cake is cut by the bride, with the help of her husband, and every guest must eat some of it. Normally the cake is cut after the toasts.

It has become the custom to send small pieces of the cake to absent friends. You can buy special little boxes for this purpose at any stationers. The bride's mother usually sees to the sending off of the boxes a day or two after the ceremony.

There is no set time for the guests to depart, though there is one firm rule: no-one must leave until the bride and groom have departed.

They must make a tour of the room, thanking everyone for coming to their wedding, and saying goodbye before they leave for their honeymoon.

It is perhaps not strictly a part of wedding etiquette, but who-pays-for-what is important.

The bride's father, in fact, pays for almost everything. He provides the invitations, the reception, the cars, the bride's dress. He is not required to pay for the bridesmaids' dresses, though the bride often makes a gift of these. The bridegroom pays for church fees or licence, for the bridesmaids' presents and of course for the honeymoon. Sometimes he will also make a gift to his best man to mark the occasion.

And when he returns from his honeymoon he will reimburse the best man for any out-of-pocket expenses he has incurred.

You will notice that the bride's mother seems to have very little to do at the ceremony or reception. This is because all her hard work will have been put in beforehand and behind the scenes. She will obviously have done most of the work arranging the reception, and of course she will have supervised the sending out of invitations, writing thank-you letters and so on. Not forgetting the help and advice she will have given in the providing of the bride's wedding attire and trousseau.

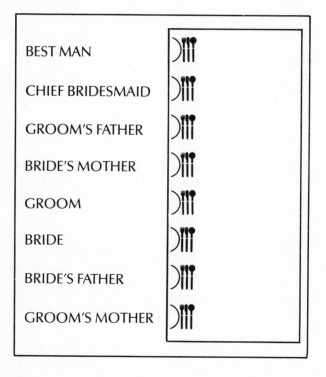

BEST MAN

CHIEF BRIDESMAID

GROOM'S FATHER

BRIDE'S MOTHER

GROOM

BRIDE

BRIDE'S FATHER

GROOM'S MOTHER

The bride's sisters, if they are bridesmaids or not, will have been pressed into service on similar work.

The bridegroom's family have little to do, although they should be consulted about the venue of the ceremony and the reception and so on. If they already know the bride's parents well, this presents no problems.

If they do not, then a small supper party should be arranged, with both sets of parents and the engaged couple attending.

It occasionally happens that the bride's parents are overseas, or perhaps not living. In this case her wedding arrangements should be made by her closest relatives available.

If she should have no close relatives, then the arrangements are normally taken over by the bridegroom's family.

If you require a report of the wedding in the local newspaper you should apply to the office for a wedding form. Usually the bride's family looks after this. The form is simply filled in with the name of the young couple, the names of their parents, the style and colour of the bride's dress, and so on.

This service is normally free, though sometimes the newspaper will not print a report unless a small advertisement in the marriages column is taken. This costs a few pounds only. Some local newspapers arrange to take wedding pictures. In this case they frequently print one with the wedding report.

One last word about wedding etiquette. The practice of throwing confetti or rose petals is happily dying out. It is rather vulgar and it makes a dreadful mess of the church precincts. If you are determined to do it, get the vicar's permission first, or that of the hotel manager.

Etiquette Reminders

Names to remember

Introductions

Dancing Partners

Table Plan

_____
_____
_____
_____
_____

Special Thankyous

_____
_____
_____
_____
_____

Photocalls

_____
_____
_____
_____

Newspapers

_____
_____
_____
_____

Second Marriage

If a man marries for the second time, wedding etiquette is almost exactly the same as for his first marriage. But there are differences for a woman, either widowed or divorced, who marries again.

To begin with the invitations are not sent by her parents. Normally she will find a woman friend to do this. At the wedding ceremony she does not wear a white gown, for this is reserved for maidenhood.

Nor does she have bridesmaids, though she can have either a maid or matron of honour, depending on whether the woman friend who attends her is married or not.

Speeches at a woman's second marriage are subtly different from those at first weddings. The toast to the bride and groom may still be given by the bride's father, but this is fairly unusual. He is not, after all, giving his daughter away in marriage this time.

Normally this toast will be made by a male friend, perhaps the husband of the bride's woman friend who sent the invitations for her. Or the toast may be made by the best man, if there is one.

As there is much less formality at a woman's second marriage, and as it is much more often held before the registrar, rather than in church, there is less need for a best man.

There are normally only two speeches: the proposal of the new couple's health, and the bridegroom's response.

These speeches will probably not have the same lightness and gaiety as at a first marriage. The tone needs to be a little more serious.

Remember that it is bad form to refer to the bride's earlier marriage.

Here is a typical toast at a second marriage:

'Ladies and Gentlemen.—It is a real pleasure to me to propose the health of Jean and Robert. They are both good friends of mine, and when I learned they were to join their lives together I could not have been happier. I think all of us in this room must feel the same. They are so eminently suited, if I may use a rather old-fashioned term. I am, in any case, a rather old-fashioned person and the sight of a good marriage puts happiness in my heart. Let us raise our glasses then to two of the nicest people I know. Or perhaps I might now say, one of the nicest couples I know.'

The response should be equally brief and simple. Like this:—

'Ladies and gentlemen.—It was most kind of you to say such nice things about Jean—my wife as I must learn to call her—and myself. We are both touched by the knowledge that we have so many good friends who have come here today to wish us well. We hope to welcome all of you in our new home when we have settled down. I would like to thank you all for your fine gifts, which we appreciate very much And I would like to express my special gratitude to Marion, who helped Jean so much with the wedding arrangements, and to Peter, who sorted out one or two tangles for me. On behalf of my wife and myself then, thank you.'

Notes